The
Positive Attitude
Development
Process

CORRECTIONAL INSTITUTION
SECOND EDITION

Assimilating, Accommodating, Acclimating to Change

DEVELOPED BY **Lyle Wildes**

POSITIVE ATTITUDE DEVELOPMENT GROUP
DULUTH, MINNESOTA

Positive Attitude Development Group
P.O. Box 231
Duluth, MN 55801-0231
E-mail: Lyle@wildesbraincoach.com
Web site: www.wildesbraincoach.com

The Positive Attitude Development Process
Assimilating, Accommodating, Acclimating to Change
CORRECTIONAL INSTITUTION SECOND EDITION

Printed in the United States of America

10 9 8 7 6 5 4 3 2

Library of Congress Control Number: 2008940749
ISBN-13 978-1-57025-229-7
ISBN   1-57025-229-7

POSITIVE ATTITUDE DEVELOPMENT GROUP
P.O. Box 231
Duluth, MN 55801-0231

Contents

Introduction

Dedicated to John and Lyn Clark Pegg

How to use this process

This book will help you learn the basics of the Positive Attitude Development (PAD) process. You can use it on your own or use it as a tool to help others identify their Core Values.

The introduction gives you an overall sense of our perspective on Positive Attitude Development. The chapters are designed to be read and used in order, since each chapter builds on concepts in the previous chapter(s).

At the end of each chapter are BrainGame activities—mental exercises related to the subject of the chapter. These exercises don't have right or wrong answers—they are designed to get you thinking in new ways.

When you come upon the BrainGame symbol in the text, go to the end of the chapter and complete that particular BrainGame exercise. When you've completed the exercise, go back to the text and keep reading.

Once you've completed a chapter, turn to the back of the book to read some reflections on the chapter's BrainGame exercises. Don't use the back of the book to figure out how many answers you got right. Instead think about your responses in light of the end-of-the-book reflections, and see what insights you gain.

At first, some BrainGame questions may seem strange and difficult. That is intentional. Each question is meant to require you to think differently. As you work through each BrainGame, remember that Positive Attitude Development comes only through daily repetition of powerful mental exercises.

In fact, we encourage you to use the BrainGame exercises over and over as you practice and keep building your new life.

We hope you enjoy your adventure.

I began to picture an attitude as the cloud from which our thoughts rain.
Next, I imagined thoughts nourishing the soil from which our actions grow.
And finally, I saw our actions blossoming into a positive, meaningful life.

Introduction

After six months in the Milan, Michigan, federal prison, my daily pulse rate was 101 beats per minute and I couldn't get it to slow down. One day, as my table started to shake, I was convinced there'd been a nearly impossible event: a Magnitude Six earthquake in Michigan.

I felt I was falling out of my chair and reached across the aisle to stabilize myself. Before my hand reached the other side, an inmate grabbed my arm and said, "Hey dude, you better do something or you're never going to make it out of prison alive." At that moment, I realized I was in trouble and something had to give.

Back then, I was convinced that everything in my life would be okay if things outside me (like other people and events) changed. If other people did what I thought they should do, then my stress would dissipate, peace would descend—and so would my heart rate. I was furious because those external stressors weren't changing (or staying the same) the way I wanted.

The situation seemed much worse because I was locked behind a prison fence with no way to influence the outside world—and I was convinced that the external world was causing all my pain. Everything just kept getting worse, and I was in serious trouble because it seemed like there was nothing I could do to change the situation. If none of the events and people on the outside were going to change (in spite of my expectations, desires and demands), there was no way to reduce my stress and possibly save my life!

I was at risk of dying for no medical reason. But what could I do? I was imprisoned by the government and by my own stress, anger and anxiety.

Of course, many other inmates were stressing out too. But I noticed some old timers who looked very calm. They seemed capable of dealing with losing everything they were attached to—including control of their daily activities and any ability to influence outside people and events.

I started asking the old timers, "What do you know that I don't?" They simply said, "You just have to put your life on hold until you get out and then pick up whatever pieces are left." That sounded right, but it still didn't relieve the pain of seeing everything I was attached to falling away. I was frozen in the moment of my arrest, while everyone else in my life was moving onward.

It was at this point of my incarceration that a fellow prisoner asked me to co-facilitate a positive attitude class that aimed to teach other inmates how to deal with change. While wondering what I could offer anyone about accepting change, this opportunity drove me to study the connection between change and the brain. The experience eventually gave me a new lease on life, ultimately helping me to feel free—even as I spent 18 more years behind bars. I realized the process for accepting change begins with one's attitude. As I enriched my own attitude I began to see everything, including my relationships, differently. This was huge!

For more than 18 years, in cooperation with prison staff, I've taught this Positive Attitude Development course in federal prisons at three security levels, each course running 20 weeks or more. The program was well received by inmates, with some taking the course multiple times.

For those of us who adopted PAD, life was no longer a battle that we had to fight every day. Even while we were restricted by incarceration, our lives became a journey. Instead of waiting for release to pick up the pieces, we began building a new life on the inside. This was the most freeing experience of my life. I now had control over how I felt about everything. My happiness was not based on the way events happened (whether within the prison or "on the outside"), but rather on the way I interpreted those events.

I began to picture an attitude as the cloud from which our thoughts rain. Next, I imagined thoughts nourishing the soil from which our actions grow. And finally, I saw our actions blossoming into a positive, meaningful life.

The texture and quality of our attitude determines the type of life we build for ourselves. That's the foundation of Positive Attitude Development, which can offer the beginning of a new life for each of us—no matter what our circumstances.

Lyle, your Positive Attitude Development course helped change my life. It taught me how to recognize my core values, how to look for the good in people and things, and how to see that my happiness does not depend on how people treat me—but on how I treat other people. This course was one of the most eye-opening, uplifting times in my life! Thank you so very much.

Your friend forever,
John Gelnette, former federal prisoner

POSITIVE ATTITUDE DEVELOPMENT

Awareness

ATTITUDE

There is hope.

I can change.

It's up to me.

Your brain is the hardware of your soul. It is the hardware of your very essence as a human being. You cannot be who you really want to be unless your brain works right. How your brain works determines how happy you are, how effective you feel, and how well you interact with others.

— Daniel G. Amen, M.D.
Change Your Brain, Change Your Life

In this session:

· The power of our beliefs

· Beliefs create our thoughts

· Thoughts create our actions

Feel Free to Change Your Brain

THE POSITIVE ATTITUDE DEVELOPMENT (PAD) process is based on the belief that the brain—a changeable organ—produces our behavior. To change our behavior, we need neurological reconstruction. We can think of it as remodeling our brains.

Our brain develops its own neurological networks, influenced by our unique daily experiences that trigger or inhibit our propensities. In a sense, during our time in the uterus, our DNA creates a brain ready to be programmed. Our experiences help program our neural networks as we grow through life. Our brains in turn adjust and

First, you must make sure that all the little, insignificant things in life bother you. Don't just leave it to chance. Sit down and get worked up over things that don't matter.

Next, make sure that you lose your perspective on things. At all costs, make mountains out of molehills and make crises out of the regular happenings of everyday life.

When you're done with that, get yourself in a state of worry. Make sure when you pick something to worry about, you choose something you can do absolutely nothing about. This will ensure your failure and cost you a lot of time you can't afford—and then you can worry about that, too.

When you're ready, launch out into the world of perfectionism. Condemn yourself and others for not being able to achieve an unachievable goal. When you make a mistake, rail against yourself.

After you have mastered perfectionism, you will then be ready to be right all the time. Be rigid in your rightness. Never allow for anyone else's perspectives.

The next step: never trust anyone and never believe in anyone. Look for everyone's weakness, and concentrate on that. Never think that you are good enough for anyone or anything.

Anything that happens to you must be taken personally at all times. And finally, never totally give yourself to anyone or anything.

adapt to help us address and/or survive our life experiences.

Recent research shows that we can construct new neurological pathways in our brains to improve our lives. But successful reconstruction requires us to block off the old, problematic neural activity at the same time that we create new pathways that produce our desired habits and behaviors. The old problematic pathways are well-worn and comforting in their familiarity, but they lead to negative consequences. So it takes sustained, conscious effort to go down the new, less-traveled path (especially if people around us remain on the old trail). In other words, our brains are still susceptible to defaulting to old behavior if the reconstruction is not maintained long enough to form a new habit.

To change behavior we have to change the workings of our brains—to change the processing system originally developed in response to our life experiences. With practice, we can have our brains prune the unused dendrites that reinforced our old negative behavior. We can also reinforce its new neural activity to support the behavior we want and need.

The Positive Attitude Development program (PAD) facilitates this process for personal change. It was developed by inmates serving long prison terms in medium-, low- and minimum-security federal prisons. PAD begins by raising awareness of the brain's immense power, using examples of how our brains respond when we're confronted by sudden change. We'll study this phenomenon for a simple reason: The way the brain habitually assimilates, accommodates, and acclimates to change determines the quality of life—and can even determine its longevity.

POSITIVE ATTITUDE DEVELOPMENT

Summary

The PAD process creates an awareness that our Core Values and their supporting Beliefs are the rudder of our lives.

"Ability is what you're capable of doing.

Motivation determines what you do.

Attitude determines how well you do it."

— **Lou Holtz**

The PAD process enables us to build a wonderful future through identifying virtuous personal:

Core Values,
and their supporting

Beliefs,
which creates a

Better Attitude,
and

Healthier Thoughts,
and

Constructive Actions,
and

New Habits,
building

Good Character,
which manifests into

A new destiny.

Our destiny will never change until we change our Core Values, our Supporting Beliefs, and our Attitude.

BrainGame

10-Year Peace-to-Chaos Continuum

We all live our days somewhere along a continuum between feeling life is peaceful or chaotic. Circle one of the numbers below to indicate where you were on this continuum 10 years ago.

10 years ago, where were you on this continuum?

10 years ago

| 1 | 2 | 3 | 4 | 5 | 6 | 7 | 8 | 9 | 10 |

PEACE ⟷ CHAOS

Today, where are you on this continuum, and in what direction are you headed?

Today

| 1 | 2 | 3 | 4 | 5 | 6 | 7 | 8 | 9 | 10 |

PEACE ⟷ CHAOS

BrainGame

Finding Your Core Values

Enclosed with your book is a deck of cards which you can use to help you identify your Core Values.

Each card has a word representing a value. Go through your deck and create two piles.

Using your deck of cards, please create two piles: 1) the words you value most; 2) the words you value less. Your "Liked Most" pile must be no more than twenty cards.

LIKED MOST   ### LIKED LESS

Now, remove five cards from the "Liked Most" pile you are willing to give up... Then remove five more cards from the "Liked Most" pile. List each card removed below.

1ˢᵗ FIVE CARDS REMOVED   #### 2ⁿᵈ FIVE CARDS REMOVED

_____   _____
_____   _____
_____   _____
_____   _____
_____   _____

Keep removing groups of 5 cards from the "Liked Most" pile until five words remain.

3ʳᵈ FIVE CARDS REMOVED   #### FINAL FIVE CARDS

_____   _____
_____   _____
_____   _____
_____   _____

Once completed, your Brain Coach will discuss your final five words or values. This will give you a clearer understanding of how your Core Values can change your life. For questions or more info, call your Brain Coach at (218) 481-7555.

BrainGame

Connecting the Dots

Connect all nine of these dots by using only 4 straight lines, without lifting your pen from the page. Answer, page 69.

Beliefs

Beliefs play a big role in our lives, but we're not clear about our beliefs.

Below, complete each outer circle with examples of beliefs that cause negative feelings about each action listed.

SAMPLE

Action: He bumped into me in the chow hall.

Belief: *He bumped into me on purpose because he doesn't like me.*

Action: He/she texted my girlfriend/boyfriend.

Belief:

Action: He/she talked shit about my family.

Belief:

Beliefs that cause negative feelings about actions

Action: She/he smiled at another man/woman.

Belief:

Action: She/he disrespected me.

Belief:

Action: She/he wasn't at the place we planned to meet.

Belief:

BrainGame

Beliefs & Actions

Now... Let's *connect the dots* between your "beliefs" and "actions."

Below, complete each outer circle with real-life actions you have experienced, and the beliefs that caused your negative feelings about those actions.

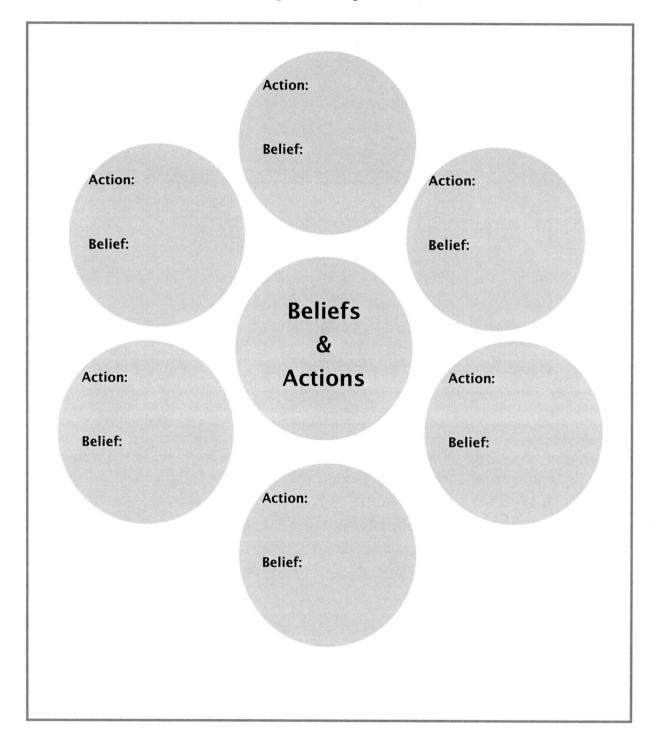

Action:

Belief:

Action:

Belief:

Action:

Belief:

Beliefs & Actions

Action:

Belief:

Action:

Belief:

Action:

Belief:

BrainGame

Three Beliefs

Write out three beliefs you do not want to give up.

1. ☐ _____

2. ☐ _____

3. ☐ _____

Put a check by the belief you experience the most resistance or conflict. Write out why others resist that belief.

_____

_____

_____

_____

_____

_____

_____

_____

_____

Attitude

The longer I live, the more I realize the impact of attitude on life. Attitude to me, is more important than facts. It is more important than the past, than education, than money, than circumstances, failures, than successes, than what people think or say or do. It is more important than appearance, giftedness, or skills. It will make or brake a company....a church....a home. The remarkable thing is we have a choice every day regarding the attitude we will embrace for that day. We cannot change our past.... we cannot change the inevitable. The only thing we can do is play on the one string we have, and that is our attitude....I am convinced that life is 10% what happens to me and 90% how I react to it. And so it is with you....we are in charge of our attitudes.

— **Charles Swindoll**

POSITIVE ATTITUDE DEVELOPMENT

Thinking

THOUGHT

I can choose.

Thoughts create behavior.

I can resist negative thinking.

In this session:

- Baseline attitude
- Plasticity
- Mental diet

Our cells are constantly eavesdropping on our thoughts and being changed by them. A bout of depression can wreak havoc with the immune system; falling in love can boost it. Despair and hopelessness raise the risk of heart attacks and cancer, thereby shortening life. Joy and fulfillment keep us healthy and extend life. This means that the line between biology and psychology can't really be drawn with any certainty. A remembered stress, which is only a wisp of thought, releases the same flood of destructive hormones as the stress itself.

—**Deepak Chopra, M.D.**
Ageless Body, Timeless Mind

Warning! Contagious! The Power of Thinking

DURING THE YEARS I TAUGHT Positive Attitude Development in prisons, people often told me that to change my destiny, I simply had to change my thinking. But the experience of teaching PAD to thousands of inmates showed me that the dynamic is more complex. If I simply try to have positive thoughts, but those thoughts are inconsistent with my existing Core Values, then I'll default back to my old thinking pattern—the same

> God, grant me the serenity to accept the persons I cannot change,
>
> The courage to change the person I can, and
>
> The wisdom to know it's me.
>
> —William C. Klatte

> What you live with, you learn.
>
> What you learn, you practice.
>
> What you practice, you become.
>
> What you become has consequences.
>
> —Earnie Larsen

> When I came to prison, I began a new life. I had to become master of my emotions because I could no longer go around out of control like I had most of my life. I was filled with hatred, envy, and strife; jealous of anyone who had the good life. Since I have been [in prison], I have learned to greet each day with love in my heart. Love can overcome anything.
>
> As I look around [this prison], I see faces of self-confidence; faces of satisfaction from taking this Positive Attitude Development class. I see faces laughing at the world with high esteem, because in spite of our situation, we will persist until we succeed.
>
> —Federal prisoner, Elkton, Ohio

that landed me in prison. We may try to keep good thoughts, but if we don't train the brain to maintain a positive attitude, then (especially at life's crucial, high-stress moments), we default to our old destructive pathways of thinking—and that makes failure our reward.

Some neurologists suggest that humans have a baseline attitude, formed during the prenatal period when billions of neural connections are made. For millions of years, the human brain has slowly evolved to help us survive and thrive in a slowly changing human environment. But over the past century, the rate of social, technological and other change in our human environment has reached breathtaking speed—a speed that continues to accelerate. The rapidly changing environment in which we currently live is different from the environment in which the brain originally emerged. So it's no surprise that we regularly feel confused and experience chaos in our lives.

This might sound as if we're condemned to discord and unhappiness. Fortunately, current research into the brain also reveals an important, refreshing reality: the brain has plasticity, which makes it possible for it to reshape itself for survival and enjoyment of life. We truly can develop our attitude because the brain is changeable—it's not locked into a static neurological landscape, preventing the possibility of a new and better life.

Because of the brain's plasticity, it can be re-formed. This is a profound concept. But we must also remember that change can go both ways; in order for us to become new people, we must police our thoughts and arrest the return of destructive thoughts we developed earlier in life.

The first requirement is changing the present mode of operation. We have to put our brain on a mental diet, replacing junk thoughts with balanced, healthy ones. This requires that our present Sense of Self be clear, tenacious, and efficient in inhibiting past negative activity, replacing the old pathways with new and desirable ones. Negative thoughts are contagious, so we have to stand guard to protect our future.

Our old habitual pathways produce loads of negative consequences: incarceration, addiction, divorce, violence, and the like. However, a single negative thought never remains alone in the human brain. It is supported by other negative thoughts. Working together on automatic pilot, they generate negative behaviors. If we aren't vigilant—now and when we are released—our old pathways will remain within, and degrade our quality of life.

The stakes are high—but so are the rewards. Let's start by examining the thoughts and actions that produced our present situation—imprisonment. We'll carefully examine our past actions, but then we'll take a further, important step. We'll ask what supporting thoughts helped create our past actions and begin to understand how the brain works. When we discover our attitude is the manifestation of our core values and their supporting beliefs we'll be at the threshold of understanding the PAD process for creating a new and exciting life. This effort requires a tenacity and efficiency at this juncture in our lives that can change the possibilities for our futures and offer us a new life. Now let's turn to our discussion and see what we can discover together about ourselves.

BrainGame: Example: Auto-Pilot Thinking

BrainGame: Your Thoughts on Automatic Pilot

The difficulty of change

Clasp your hands together with your fingers folded over each other in a natural manner. Does this feel normal or comfortable? Now shift the fingers on your right hand over one spot. Does this feel normal or comfortable?

The brain wants you to keep it (and thus you) in its default position. It works for your comfort, but not necessarily for your success—unless you change its default patterns. Changing your brain's default patterns requires putting it on a new mental diet.

BrainGame: What Are You Thinking?

Summary

This lesson teaches the process for Positive Attitude Development. It challenges our default thinking by questioning our core values and their supporting beliefs and asking how they have contributed to our present situation.

Example: Auto-Pilot Thinking

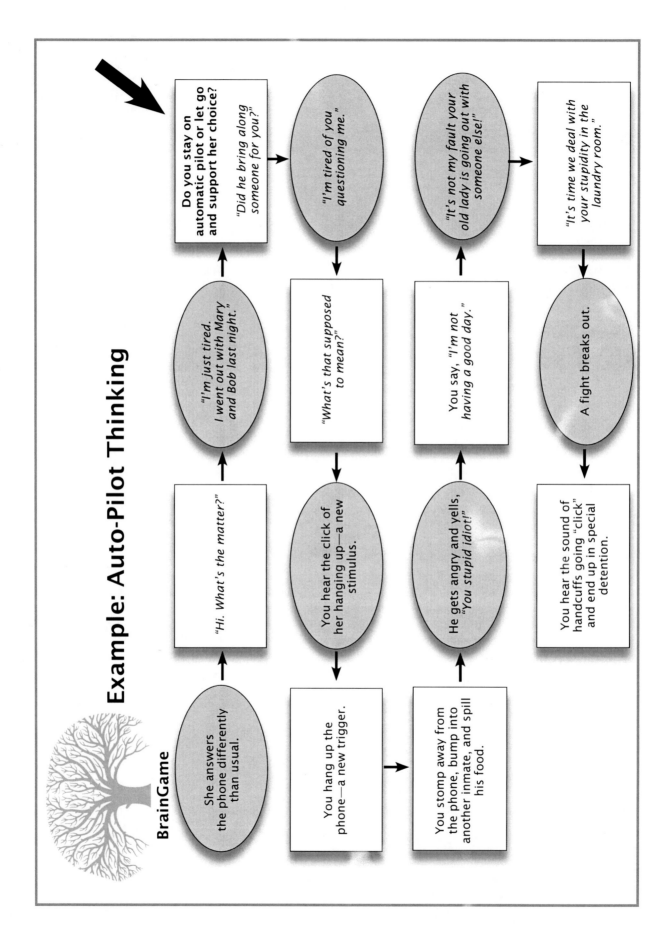

BrainGame

She answers the phone differently than usual.

→ "Hi. What's the matter?"

→ "I'm just tired. I went out with Mary and Bob last night."

→ **Do you stay on automatic pilot or let go and support her choice?** "Did he bring along someone for you?"

→ "I'm tired of you questioning me."

→ "What's that supposed to mean?"

→ You hear the click of her hanging up—a new stimulus.

→ You hang up the phone—a new trigger.

→ You stomp away from the phone, bump into another inmate, and spill his food.

→ He gets angry and yells, "You stupid idiot!"

→ You say, "I'm not having a good day."

→ "It's not my fault your old lady is going out with someone else!"

→ "It's time we deal with your stupidity in the laundry room."

→ A fight breaks out.

→ You hear the sound of handcuffs going "click" and end up in special detention.

BrainGame

Your Thoughts on Automatic Pilot

Use this space to describe a situation in your own life like the one demonstrated on p. 22. Draw boxes to illustrate what you said, thought and did; and draw ovals for what other people said or did.

BrainGame

What Are *You* Thinking?

Write down your thoughts about the questions below. Use another sheet of paper if you need it. After you're done, take a look at page 69 to see our thoughts on the subject.

Those who cannot remember the past are condemned to repeat it.—**George Santayana**

What's the first thought that comes to mind when you see each of these words?

Anger _____

Betrayal _____

Joy _____

Compassion _____

Forgiveness _____

What do you think it means to begin a new life?

_____

How can you begin a new life in prison?

_____

Do you need to forget the past to begin a new life?

_____

How important is forgiveness in beginning a new life?

_____

Are there any actions that you just can't forgive? If so, what are they?

_____

What purpose does it serve to bury the hatchet if you're going to mark the spot?

_____

If we do not learn from the past, are we condemned to repeat it?

_____

POSITIVE ATTITUDE DEVELOPMENT

Trust

In this session:

· Conceive, believe, achieve

· SNIOP / SPIOP

· Contagious thoughts

ACTIONS

Thoughts create actions.

Repetitive actions.

Create habits.

Trust That It Works

THE MOST IMPORTANT ELEMENT for change is learning to trust the universe. Why trust the universe? Because it's pretty reliable. If we heat water (to 212° Fahrenheit or 100° Celsius at sea level), it will boil and turn into steam. If we cool it down (to 32° Fahrenheit or 0° Celsius at sea level), it will freeze. We can boil or freeze H_2O over and over again for the rest of our lives, and we'll always get the same result. The same holds true for millions of other chemical, physical and biological reactions that we can rely on in the animal, plant and mineral worlds.

Likewise, if you take the same actions over and over again, in the same or similar situations, it is extremely likely that you will get the same result. If you get angry and call your spouse or partner a nasty name, the odds are high that she or he will be upset in response.

Do it a third time and what happens?

We have to trust that, in our universe, like attitudes produce like thoughts and vice versa. A negative attitude tends to produce negative thoughts and negative thoughts tend to produce negative

My name is Kim. My story begins when I was released from prison. Before I got out, I completed a drug and alcohol program and was making a fresh, new start in life. I started by hanging out on the beach enjoying the sun and people and feeling alive and free, taking time for myself, something I'd never done before. After getting a job at the concession stand on the beach, I was in heaven, making a few bucks and being on the beach daily. Then with summer almost over, I knew I needed to find another job. I found work at a janitorial service, making $6.25 an hour. Not much, but a job all the same. I put my best work forward and it paid off.

After a few weeks of cleaning bathrooms and offices, I was offered a job building houses. But when I tried to resign from the janitorial company, they said they liked my work and couldn't let me go. Instead, they made me a manager in charge of 40 employees at 13 separate buildings, dealing with customer complaints, ordering supplies, etc., etc. Being a boss was something I didn't expect in my future, having just left prison as a convicted felon. It just goes to show, keep your head up, push forward, and good things will happen.

I was a good boss. I used your positive attitude approach with my employees and customers. Our monthly complaint rate fell from between 40 and 60 to just a few. I did this by personally speaking to the people and directing solutions to their complaints in person, then following through by talking to the

behaviors—which produce negative actions and negative consequences. This is a basic idea that may be simplistic, but it's nevertheless true.

I'm asking you to trust that PAD is a process that will develop healthy beliefs, attitudes, thoughts and actions. If you're tenacious and courageous about PAD, you'll begin to experience the wonders and mysteries of life—catching your imagination and spirit and filling your life with fun and excitement.

Do you believe that what the mind can conceive and believe, it can achieve? I do, because I've seen remarkable evidence of it.

Take former insurance executive Morris Goodman, whom I met when he spoke to PAD participants in our prison. In 1981, Morris crashed his single-engine aircraft, breaking vertebrae, damaging his spinal cord. He was left paralyzed from the neck down. By the time rescuers brought Morris to the hospital, physicians were amazed he was still alive. The only way he could communicate was by blinking his eyes once for "yes" and twice for "no."

Before emergency surgery, doctors told Morris that his chances for survival were slim. Afterward, he still couldn't move, breathe, or eat on his own. But, Morris explains, "After I lived through the surgery, I set a goal to walk out of the hospital in six months. My sister made a chart of letters to help me communicate. To make myself understood to the outside world, my sister and I developed a system of blinks that indicated the letter I wanted, and through this very slow process, I put together words and sentences to express my thoughts and decisions. Nothing was going to stop me from recovering."

He overcame astounding odds in the process. For example, the injuries left Morris' diaphragm muscle unable to expand and contract his lungs—

he had to be tethered to a breathing machine. So, he set out to teach himself how to use his still-working stomach muscles to do the job instead. He mastered this seemingly impossible feat and succeeded in breathing without any machines.

Morris had to relearn how to swallow, speak and perform many other basic bodily functions. Doctors and other professionals told him that such a complete recovery was impossible. Morris responded by asking, "Why?" When they said they'd never seen anyone do it before, Morris decided to set his goals higher than what others saw for him or expected from him.

When Morris met with us in prison, he was adamant that it took more than determination and hard work to recover. Crucial to his recovery was visualization: seeing himself totally recovered— and not settling for "just walking out of the hospital."

His method wasn't easy: Morris explains that it required putting his mind on a strict mental diet of only positive beliefs, attitudes, and thoughts. It also meant finding and bringing together people (like his sister) who believed as he did—that the cells of his body were eavesdropping on the positive, recovery-focused thoughts of his mind— and responding accordingly.

This last part of Morris' method helps illustrate the important principles of "SNIOP" and "SPIOP." As humans, we are Susceptible to the Negative Influences of Other People (SNIOP). You'd be right to think that prison is one of the best places to observe SNIOP. After all, bad decisions land most felons in the joint, where all that negativity easily feeds on itself.

But our experience with PAD in prison also shows how much we humans are also Susceptible to the Positive Influences of Other People (SPIOP). Key

employee responsible and checking later to make sure the area was cleaned properly.

After 13 months of continuous service, never missing a day of work, my job was eliminated, with the company claiming I hadn't disclosed my complete felony record at the time of hiring. I'd given the H.R. department a complete copy of my record from the courthouse and talked about the nature of my felonies with the person hiring me. In the end it didn't make any difference. I started collecting un-employment and looking for a new job.

After close to three months of not finding a job (and not trying too hard to find one), I found construction work. The men on the crew were typical construction types, all drinkers. Coming from a long history of dysfunctional drinking myself, I did what I said I'd never do again. After a ten-hour day one Friday, we all stopped at a bar. I thought, "I'm one of the men and I can handle this." After most of the guys left, I was still there with my boss talking shop and getting drunk. It was around 1:00 a.m. when I got into my truck to make my way home. I was pulled over, resulting in my sixth drunk driving offense. My life, my woman, my kids and my positive attitude were put on hold. As a result, I'm at Gordon Correctional Center in.

I hope this helps others to see that the problem is always there and that even the strong fall. I'm picking up the pieces once again. I'd love to start building that positive, untouchable feeling again—and then share it with others here at Gordon.

—**Kim Modrow**

Other people call you Nicotine, but we've been together all these years, so I'm going to call you Nicky. I've come to realize that you've misled me for so long about what you are to me and what you can do for me.

You remind me a lot of some relationships I've had before with other people—where I thought only of what they were like in the beginning: all the love, the good times, how we did everything together, and how hard it was to continue without that person. In the past, when I wanted to let you go (much like my relationships with people), you would manipulate me and say, "Let's talk about this tomorrow." But I've put this off so long already.

The truth is, Nicky; my relationship with you is killing me. You sure aren't my friend because friends don't leave you coughing or make you unable to breathe. When I sleep at night, I hear what you've done to my lungs—the wheezing. You cause me nothing but harm and unhappiness and unless I end this relationship with you, you'll cause my death.

I know I'll have a period in my life that I may even grieve over not having you, but that will pass. It will go away and I'll see that I'm so very, very much better off without you. Good-bye, Nicky; don't come back. I don't need you anymore

— **Stewert Van Maasdam**
Duluth Federal Prison Camp

to the success of PAD in prison (as in any other environment—including those you will inhabit upon your release) is to actively find support from other like-minded people. And, from what we've learned so far about the brain, I mean "like-minded" quite literally.

Take my friend Stu whose story you read on the left. He was a lifelong smoker stuck in prison. After his PAD training, fellow participants supported Stewert as he took the major step of breaking free of his nicotine addiction by changing his beliefs, thoughts and attitudes about the problem.

BrainGame: Susceptibility Scan

BrainGame: Beliefs, Thoughts, and Actions

Summary

This lesson shows the power of a persistently positive attitude—even when confronted with sudden, extreme change. It reveals the concrete connection between our thoughts and our physical lives.

BrainGame

Susceptibility Scan

Write down your thoughts about the questions below. Use another sheet of paper if you need it. After you've completed your answers, take a look at page 71 to see some of our thoughts on the subject.

Write out the words associated with the letters below.

S _____   S _____

N _____   P _____

I _____   I _____

O _____   O _____

P _____   P _____

How did Morris Goodman repel SNIOP in his recovery?

_____

_____

Morris put himself on a strict mental diet—but it wasn't a diet of deprivation, like a weight-loss program uses. What kind of nourishment did Morris feed his brain while on his mental diet?

_____

_____

Give some examples of negative influences you have to overcome in prison.

_____

_____

What negative influences, if any, will you experience after your release?

_____

_____

BrainGame

Beliefs, Thoughts, and Actions

Write down your thoughts about the questions below. Use another sheet of paper if you need it. After you've completed your answers, take a look at page 72 to see some of our thoughts on the subject.

What do you think would have happened to you if you had been in an accident like Morris Goodman had?

_____

_____

_____

_____

_____

What would your beliefs, attitude and thoughts have been in that situation?

_____

_____

_____

_____

_____

What is the difference between those beliefs, attitude and thoughts and the ones that Morris seems to have in his recovery?

_____

_____

_____

_____

_____

POSITIVE ATTITUDE DEVELOPMENT

Seven Seconds

HABITS

I can't change the past.

I will stay in the now.

Because now is all I have.

In this session:

· The past is history

· The future is a mystery

· Now is our present

The Seven-Second Life

AS PRISONERS, many areas of our lives are managed by others (like the prison staff) without our permission. However, despite our incarceration, important portions of our lives—especially our thoughts—remain to be managed by us. For example, some 60,000 thoughts pass through our brains every day. 95% of our thoughts are the same every day. We keep repeating the same thoughts over and over every day.

Think about how many things a prison guard can make you do every day. Five? Twenty-five? Even 100 demands are puny compared to the 60,000 thoughts you control each day. Nevertheless, our thoughts are often negative ones, like thoughts bemoaning the way our lives are managed by outside circumstances—something we did before we ever got near a prison. If we really can control our thoughts, why would so many of them be negative? It's because of the way we visualize our situation.

The thoughts we have every 24 hours constitute a strongly rushing stream. That stream is our

When Mark Twain was an old man, a reporter asked him: "How do you remain calm and reassured in the declining years of your life?"

Twain answered: "I select two days of each week to be free of worry."

"Oh," replied the reporter. "That's an interesting strategy. Which two days do you chose?"

Twain answered, "Yesterday and tomorrow."

core of life that we can and must begin to manage more effectively.

To live fully, we have to narrow our attention to a controllable span of experience and time, aka the present. The secret is to understand that we will never have a better past. The past is what it is and that's not going to change. The only thing about the past that can change is the way that we see and use past experiences in our lives today. We can change the pathways that produced our past actions and their consequences.

To live fully in the present moment requires that we don't live in the future, either. We have to avoid imagining the future in ways that destroy our window of life or daily portal of experience. We can prepare for the future, but we can't live tomorrow until it's here. If we try to, we miss the present.

Here's the bottom line: We can't change the past or the future; the universe doesn't allow it. Trying to change the past or the future is a waste of our time and energy— just like we'd be wasting our time and energy trying to get water to boil or freeze at 85°. No amount of effort is going to make it happen.

We'll begin learning how to live in the

moment by zooming in on a few drops of our gushing, often turbulent, stream of thoughts: those drops of thought we're having during a seven-second window of our own experience.

BrainGame: Zeroing in on Now

BrainGame: Fear Factors

Homework: Use BrainGame: Zeroing in on Now three times a day, every day until the next session.

Summary

This lesson shows the importance of shrinking our attention to seven seconds: two seconds that are fading, the three we are in, and the two that are approaching. This moment of eternity is where we can fully live. This lesson shows how to participate in this moment of eternity and enjoy life as it comes.

Zeroing in on Now

What is your present stream of thought?

Time yourself for 10 seconds and quickly jot down key words that reflect the stream of thoughts you have during that 10-second period.

See page 73 for our thoughts on these issues.

Eternity

Birth   Now-7 Seconds   *Death*

Eternity

Speed Write-Down 1

_____   _____   _____

_____   _____   _____

_____   _____   _____

Speed Write-Down 2

_____   _____   _____

_____   _____   _____

_____   _____   _____

Speed Write-Down 3

_____   _____   _____

_____   _____   _____

_____   _____   _____

BrainGame

Fear Factors

Write down your thoughts about the questions below. When you have completed your answers, look on page 73 for our thoughts about these issues.

The biggest killers of time are: Procrastination, Doubt, and Fear. Fear can be defined as False Evidence Appearing Real or Fantasized Experiences Appearing Real.

How do you define fear?

F _____

E _____

A _____

R _____

Describe a time when false or fantasized experiences appeared real in your life.

_____

_____

If you knew you were going to die tonight, what would you do with the rest of today?

_____

_____

_____

How would your loved ones describe you at your funeral?

_____

_____

_____

POSITIVE ATTITUDE DEVELOPMENT

Persistence

◄ CHARACTER ►

I can succeed.

I can accomplish.

I can live smart.

In this session:

· Failure is not genetic?

· Persistence!

· Vocabulary diet

The Power of Persistence

IS FAILURE GENETIC, or are people conditioned to fail? There's no evidence that failure is wired into our DNA, our blood, our heritage, or our biological makeup. After more than two decades in prison, I know countless stories of men who were conditioned to fail, expected to fail, and frequently resisted taking even the simplest steps toward success.

One example is a former gang member, my friend and fellow inmate Shane. By the time Shane got to prison, he expected to fail in life. When he faced failure, he didn't go to others for help, because he believed the world had either turned against him or given up on him. Shane was convinced that nobody was interested in helping him.

After working on positive attitude development, however, he began trying tenacity and trusting that he could succeed. For example, Shane decided to conscientiously complete all of the tasks expected by the parole board. He doggedly followed their recommendations, anticipating that this would

O.K. So I lost my Wonder-Bread job. Did I let that stop me or slow me down? Hell NO! I was looking for a job when I got that one! So I hit the bricks (in my car, of course) and found a job as a plumber for $10.00 an hour with all the bennies. And I like my job. The owner said I impressed her with my honesty by laying everything out on the table. I was in prison for 14 years. It was a dope charge. I knew nothing about plumbing.

But on the other hand, I'm a hard worker. I show up on time. I went to college while in prison. I was part of the Youth Awareness Program. I taught recovery and relapse classes for over three years. I attended PAD classes for over 60 weeks. And on and on.

So anyway, I got the job and I like the job.

—Monte Apfel

lead directly to the shortening of his sentence.

But after repeated appearances before the board, Shane still wasn't paroled. He was denied because the parole board could find no record of Shane completing one of his required classes. Shane always assured them that he'd taken it, but the board didn't budge. He left these hearings frustrated and angry at the world.

The next time Shane was eligible to go before the parole board, his frustration hadn't dissipated. He told the prison staff, "Why bother going back there? I do what they tell me to do, and it doesn't make any difference—they don't believe me. The 90-minute trip will be a waste of my time, your time and the gas."

Despite Shane's objection, his case manager signed him up for an appointment anyway. So Shane once again told the parole board that he'd followed all of their instructions. But the board still couldn't find a record of Shane completing that one certain class.

Shane felt his frustration bubbling over again. He looked over at the staff from his prison. They knew he'd completed the class, but they weren't doing anything. So Shane nudged one of them and said, "Isn't there any way you can look this up somewhere and show them that I took the class?"

At that, one of the staffers went over to a nearby computer. Within ten minutes, she found the official document proving Shane's completion of the class, printed it out, and handed it over to the parole board. The parole board promptly cut the final year from Shane's sentence, and he was released less than two weeks later.

Even though Shane hadn't fully realized it then, he'd begun to cast aside his old beliefs that people were out to get him, the world had no use for him, and no one would help him.

Despite being very angry and frustrated in the moment, Shane had asked for help. Help was there—and he won a year of freedom just by showing tenacity for ten minutes longer than he'd planned.

When a setback (like being denied parole) happens, it may feel like an insurmountable failure. At such times, we have a couple of choices: giving up to stay where we are, or giving up to move on. Throwing up our hands in despair keeps us in a cycle of failure, being weak and feeling worthless. The stronger, healthier option is to adopt a different course: letting go of setbacks and accepting them as temporary, rather than dwelling on them as if they are permanent. In fact, something that appears to be failure is often a step along the road to success.

Hall-of-Famer Barry Sanders (1989–1998) has the third most rushing yards in NFL history. Sanders also holds the NFL record for the most carries for negative yardage (according to Sports Illustrated: The Football Book, it's 336 carries for losses of 952 yards). But lost yardage was central to what made Sanders' running style so electric and effective. His Detroit Lions team was usually weak; when he ran into resistance at the line, he reversed field—often retreating 10 to 20 yards in order to gain 5 or 10—or a whole lot more.

Reggie Jackson has the most career postseason home runs: 18. He's Top 10 for career homers in the pre-steroid era (563). He also has the most strikeouts in a career: 2,597. Averaging about 500 at-bats a season over 21 years, Jackson spent five full seasons striking out, and a little more than one season hitting homers. Which statistic is Jackson remembered for?

BrainGame: A Vocabulary Diet

BrainGame: Determining Your Success

BrainGame: Through Valleys to Peaks

BrainGame: Tracking Your Personal Development

Summary

This lesson shows the importance of persistence, because both failure and success are inevitable parts of life. It shows ways to repel negative thoughts so that we can reach our goals.

BrainGame

A Vocabulary Diet

Write down your thoughts about the questions below. Use another sheet of paper if you need it. After you've completed your answers, see page 74 to see some of our thoughts on the subject.

How are you tested or challenged every day?

_____

_____

Certain words or phrases promote failure. What words or phrases have you heard other people use that you think have promoted failure in their lives?

_____

_____

What words or phrases have you used that you think have promoted failure in your life?

_____

_____

What things do you tell yourself that erode your motivation?

_____

_____

What words or phrases do you need to remove from your vocabulary to help you reach your goals?

_____

_____

Which of these statements do you believe?

A. Failure is genetic.   B. We become conditioned to fail.

BrainGame

Determining Your Success

Write down your thoughts about the questions below. Use another sheet of paper if you need it. After you've completed your answers, see page 75 to see some of our thoughts on the subject.

What have you given up on in the past that, upon reflection, you know you could have accomplished if you'd persisted?

_____

_____

What are some small steps you've taken to reach a goal?

_____

_____

What's a positive way to perceive obstacles and adversity?

_____

_____

Is life like the Super Bowl—does your winning depend on someone else losing?

_____

_____

What other ways might there be to perceive success?

_____

_____

BrainGame

Through Valleys to Peaks

Ohio State Head Football Coach Jim Tressel says that life's low points are necessary; it's in the lows, when you face obstacles, that you get what you need to go higher. Coach Tressel came to the federal prison in Elkton, Ohio, and explained how a player develops—or fails to develop—over four years.

Getting to this level requires Positive Attitude Development

Success requires peaks and valleys for him to stay in the game.

But other teams also continue countering his newest skills.

He understands what success requires of him. He reaches new heights.

Even elite players must go through a valley to improve.

He pushes to improve his skills even more, playing at an elite level.

Learning new skills is hard & exhausting. Other teams continue to counter his new strengths. He might think this is his best.

He uses the new challenge to improve his skills & play at a higher level.

Other teams learn to counter his strengths, so he has less success. He might give up here.

Player arrives as the best in his high school; thinks he's hot (and will often play hot).

BrainGame

Tracking Your Personal Development

See page 76 for our thoughts about these issues.

What are some examples of what you've learned in some of the peaks and valleys of your life?

Peaks

_____

_____

_____

_____

_____

_____

_____

Valleys

_____

_____

_____

_____

_____

_____

_____

If we never screw up, we never learn life's most important lessons.
Remember to honor your mistakes.

—Joe Kelly

What I discovered was that happiness is not something that happens. It is not the result of good fortune or random chance. It is not something money can buy or power command. It does not depend on outside events, but, rather, how we interpret them. Happiness, in fact, is a condition that must be prepared for, cultivated, and defended privately by each person. People who learn to control inner experience will be able to determine the quality of their lives, which is as close as any of us can come to being happy.

— **Mihaly Csikszentmihalyi**
Flow: The Psychology of Optimal Experience

POSITIVE ATTITUDE DEVELOPMENT

My Emotions

◆ **CHARACTER** ◆

My beliefs give my experiences value.

When I change my beliefs I change my character.

I can remain calm no matter what happens.

Emotional Thunderstorms

AN EMOTION CAN BE DEFINED as the process by which the brain determines or computes the value of a stimulus. Other aspects of emotions then follow this computation.

Western culture tends to describe destructive emotion as one that results in harm to oneself, others or property. Eastern culture describes it as one that disrupts the equilibrium of one's inner peace.

Here's how emotion works in our brains and bodies. Say you hit your thumb with a hammer. Nerves in your thumb, hand and arm send a pain signal to your brain. You almost immediately experience pain and yank your thumb away (your body's instinctive response to removing a hurt extremity from the source of danger). The progress of events— thumb tissue is injured, nerves fire, brain receives signal, muscles contract to quickly move the thumb—are steps of biochemical changes in the body's internal physiology, your body's instinctive response to something it perceives as a crisis.

> **In this session:**
> - How are your feelings hurt?
> - Refractory period
> - The meaning of events

43

In these initial nanoseconds, emotions haven't kicked in yet. The overt bodily responses and associated pain are the advance guard of emotional responsiveness. It's only afterward (remember, we're talking nanoseconds) that a feeling emerges. This is the time during which you become aware that your brain has determined that something important is happening. Only then are your emotions aroused. In the case of hitting your thumb with a hammer, you're likely (although certainly not required) to start feeling anger and emotional pain.

Like the initial instinctive chain reaction, aroused emotions also trigger biochemical reactions in the brain that generate action—for example, jumping up and down and screaming some four-letter words. In reaction to both the preconscious response and the emotional response, we do things to cope with (or capitalize on) the external event that triggers us.

Next, there's a period of time that passes between the onset of the intense emotional reaction and the return to a state of relative emotional balance. This refractory period can last seconds, minutes or years. Positive Attitude Development helps reduce the intensity and length of the refractory period.

As hard as it may be to imagine, we can develop an attitude that delivers a different, unexpected emotional response. For example, after much training a Zen master might respond with laughter ("How silly of me to hit my thumb with a hammer!"), expressions of gratitude ("Thank goodness I didn't break the bone!") or no emotion at all ("This event has no meaning to me").

The cycle of our emotional reactions to situations, people, or events is not pre-determined or carved in stone. (After all, Zen masters are humans, too.) Through our life experience, we learn ways to respond to various stimuli. Remember Session 1?

Our brain develops its own neurological network, influenced by our unique daily experiences that trigger or inhibit our propensities. In a sense, during our time in the uterus, our DNA creates a brain ready to be programmed. Our experiences help program our neural networks as we grow through life. Our brains in turn adjust and adapt to help us address and/or survive our life experiences.

Sometimes, emotional reactions we would label destructive (like denial or apathy) work as short-term survival strategies to get us through immediate crises, especially when we're children. However, our past lessons about emotions are often inadequate for our present situations. What worked as a survival skill in childhood doesn't always work in adult society—even the society of prison. The old attitude and emotional response habits must now be arrested and replaced with new constructive responses.

How do we do this? Once again, it comes down to developing new core values, beliefs, and a positive attitude at which point our behavior (and its consequences) become healthy.

If the hammer doesn't hit your thumb very hard, then your pain (and the resulting anger) is likely to pass quickly—perhaps in a matter of seconds. You could be laughing about it five minutes later. This is because emotions come and go. When it comes to emotions, the sage is right when he says, "This, too, shall pass." However, we have to remember that this, too, shall pass applies to constructive emotions just as much as it does to destructive emotions. The attitude behind an emotion determines how long and how intensely that emotion will stick around. If you don't feed the supporting thoughts, the emotion will pass, no matter what it is.

When hammer and thumb make contact, getting angry and cursing may serve us well in the very short term. A yell and a hop can release the adrenalin-fueled muscle tension that's part of the body's instinctive response to pain. However, continued anger and curses are no help. They keep us stuck in a moment of emotional thunderstorm, even though the actual rain, thunder and lightening are long gone. It's as if we pull out our umbrella in the storm, but even after it's passed and the sun is shining, we hold on to the umbrella—and we keep the rain falling beneath it. We cut off our access to fully experiencing the moments happening afterward, including their potential for stimulating positive emotions within us. Too many of us feed our anger more often than necessary and stay angry far longer than will serve our best interests and well-being.

Remember that our thinking stream passes at enormous speed—60,000 thoughts a day. If we stop and just observe the stream, we remain calm. But if we grab on to any one negative thought, we're off on a roller coaster ride. We feed that thought with others like it, and we're emotionally hooked. If we don't interrupt the pattern and detach—cold turkey—from the negative thoughts, we can spend minutes, hours, or even days, inflating the problem and knocking our lives off course.

You've seen it happen in prison. Luis says something to Jerry and you can actually see Jerry get hooked—his body tenses, his stance alters, his tone of voice changes. In a split second, Jerry is caught by rage—and within a few minutes, his behavior might land him in the hole.

You can probably see similar patterns around you at work or home. These knee-jerk reactions may seem unavoidable, but we actually do have other choices. Positive attitude lies in unhooking—that is, not getting attached to the thoughts either speeding or crawling by. Emotional detachment (which is not the same as apathy or amputation) is where balance, serenity and peace lie.

What we say and do influences how we feel as much as how we feel influences what we say and do. Feelings and actions reinforce each other.

BrainGame: Recognizing an Emotional Pattern

Hitting that thumb with the hammer is emotionally meaningless until we interpret the event and give it meaning. The meaning one person gives that event may be very different from the meaning someone else gives it; compare the angry, cursing guy to the Zen master.

When someone says or does something that hurts our feelings, what is it that hurts?

Our emotional reaction may reach—or exceed—our emotional reaction after the hammer bruises our thumb. But when our feelings are hurt, no skin, muscles or nerves are damaged. So what hurts, and why?

Most of us know or have heard about a prisoner who committed suicide, whether at their own hands or through suicide-by-cop. Most of us can understand someone wanting to kill himself while living in captivity, a situation that appears hopeless.

But what about people who live in everyday society, where their freedom isn't restricted? Clearly, some of us humans despair no matter where we live. For me, a perfect example is Mr. G., who taught at one of the federal prisons where I used to live. Mr. G. always bragged about the beautiful woman he'd married. Then, one day, his wife left him. He came to work and broke down in tears during class. The prisoners told him, "C'mon, get it together. You can get another job or move someplace else. You've got your freedom, man! When one of us loses our woman, we have reason to be frustrated because there's no one else on the market! You can find another one."

However, Mr. G. had built his entire Sense of Self on having this pretty woman in his life. Rationally, he should have been grateful for his freedom and the options available to him—especially after spending every work day among men with severely restricted freedom and options. Nevertheless, his negative thoughts and faulty beliefs took over. He was living his life for another person; when she left him, he thought and believed that the meaning of his life had disappeared as well. He couldn't get his

thoughts in control, even though he had opportunity and freedom. The next day, he killed himself.

The point is this: Our beliefs, attitudes and thoughts determine our emotions and behavior. When we change them, then the emotional reactions (along with their intensity and duration) change, too.

BrainGame: Recognizing Your Emotional Pattern

Our emotions have a kind of cycle or logarithm. Happy, sad, indifferent—feelings happen during the day like seasons move through the year. The logarithm is slightly different in each person, but there tends to be a consistent pattern for how the pharmacy in our brains distributes the chemicals that affect our moods. It's our privilege to learn how to alter that cycle through the mental exercises of PAD, so that we can improve the functioning of the brain's pharmacy. Knowing that the brain has plasticity, we can rework the chemical construction of our moods.

Summary

This lesson is about understanding the cycle of emotions and why we experience various moods. The paradigm of PAD brings forth the idea that chemistry, hormones and neurological activities are the precursors to feelings and behavior—and that we can alter them.

Your own moods can be extremely deceptive. They can, and probably do, trick you into believing your life is far worse than it really is. When you're in a good mood, life looks great. You have perspective, common sense, and wisdom. In good moods, things don't feel so hard, problems seem less formidable and easier to solve. When you're in a good mood, relationships seem to flow and communication is easy. If you are criticized, you take it in stride.

On the contrary, when you're in a bad mood, life looks unbearably serious and difficult. You have very little perspective. You take things personally and often misinterpret those around you, as you impute malignant motives into their actions.

— **Richard Carlson, PhD**
Don't Sweat the Small Stuff...and It's All Small Stuff

Recognizing an Emotional Pattern

This is a typical example of a prisoner repeating old emotional patterns that translate into "auto-pilot" thinking and action that lead inevitably to difficulty.

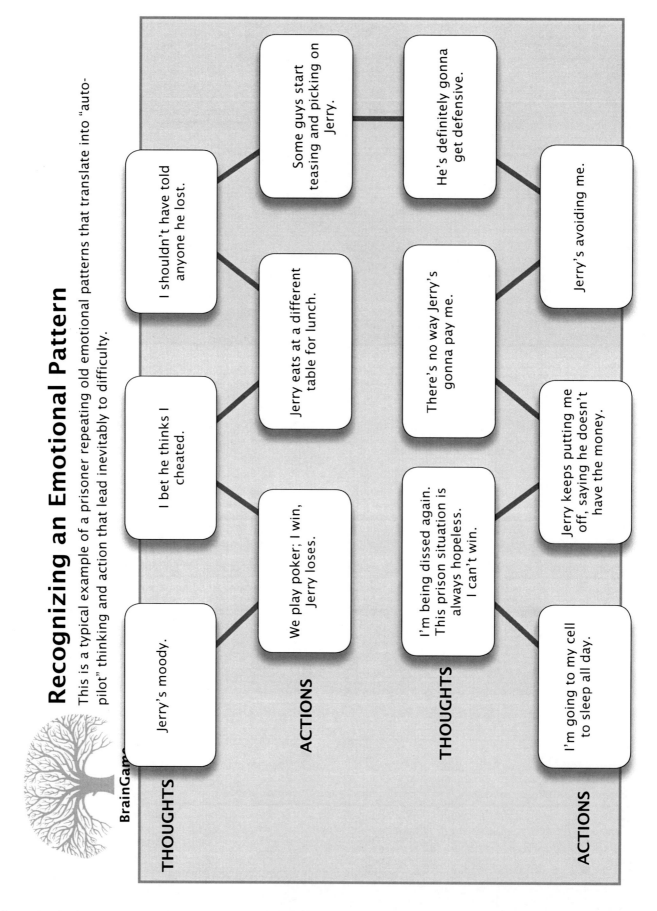

THOUGHTS

Jerry's moody.

I bet he thinks I cheated.

I shouldn't have told anyone he lost.

Some guys start teasing and picking on Jerry.

ACTIONS

We play poker; I win, Jerry loses.

Jerry eats at a different table for lunch.

He's definitely gonna get defensive.

THOUGHTS

I'm being dissed again. This prison situation is always hopeless. I can't win.

There's no way Jerry's gonna pay me.

Jerry's avoiding me.

ACTIONS

I'm going to my cell to sleep all day.

Jerry keeps putting me off, saying he doesn't have the money.

BrainGame

Recognizing Your Emotional Pattern

Use this chart to plot out a time when your repetition of old emotional patterns translated into "auto-pilot" thinking and action leading inevitably to difficulty.

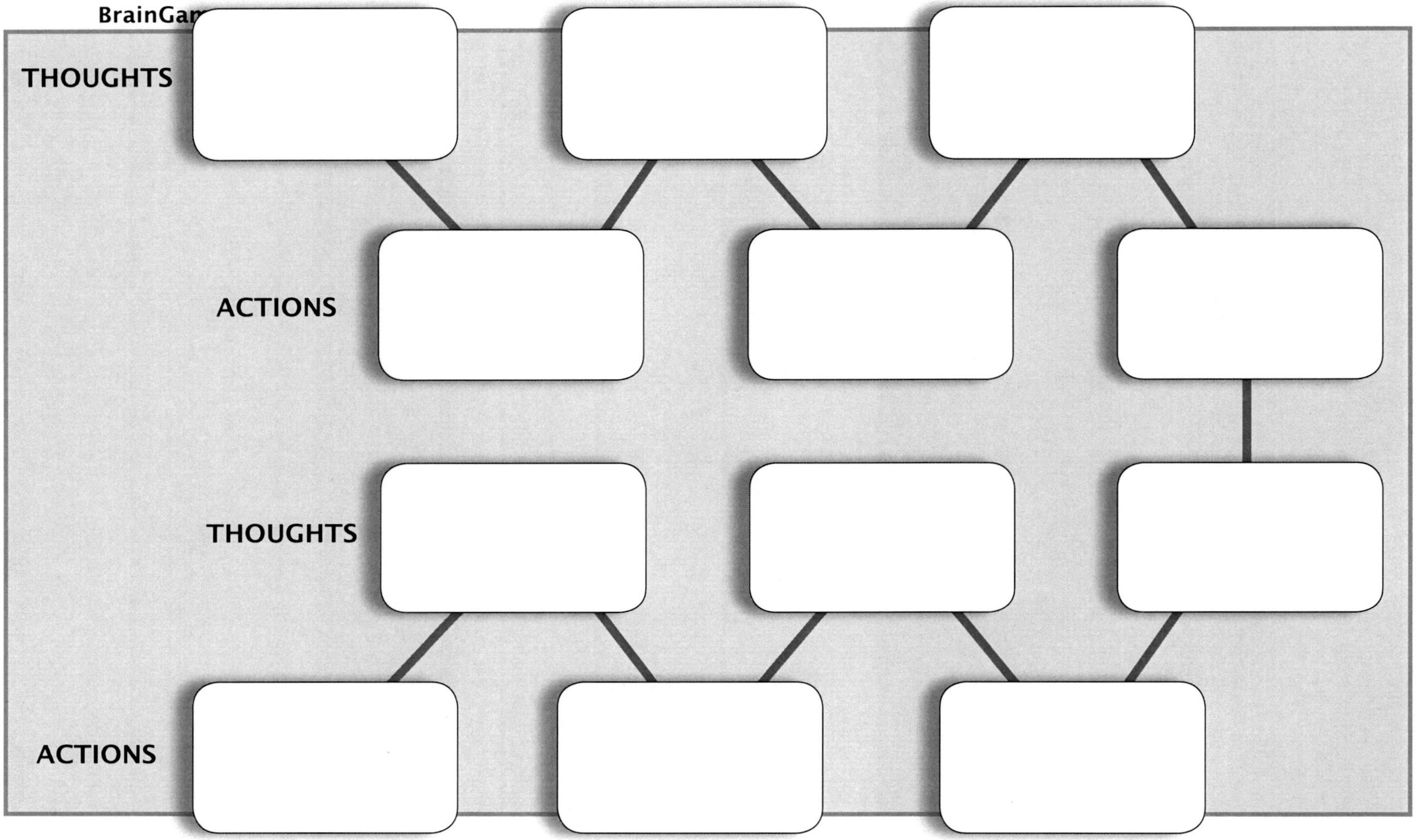

BrainGar

THOUGHTS

ACTIONS

THOUGHTS

ACTIONS

Whether you think you can,

Or you think you can't —

Either way, you're right.

— **Henry Ford**

Focus

Don't be a wandering generality; be a meaningful specific.

—Zig Ziglar

I can let go.

I can determine my future.

And my destiny.

In this session:

· The difference between a goal and a wish

· How and why set goals

· What goals accomplish along the way

Setting Goals

IF YOU'RE OUTSIDE ON A SUNNY DAY, moving a magnifying glass all around, it doesn't serve much purpose. But held very still and focus it on something flammable, and then what happens? That same magnifying glass can burn your house down.

Did you spend more time planning your wedding than you did planning your marriage? Have you spent more time planning vacations than planning your life? If so, you're not alone—even though such an approach to planning makes little sense. As we start to develop our beliefs, attitude, and positive thoughts, we have to ask, what are we going to do with them? How will we make smart use of them? The next step is to put our beliefs, attitude, and thoughts to work in achieving positive goals in our lives.

After a few weeks of taking the PAD course, a prisoner once told me, "It sounds like you're teaching us not to ask why something happened,

When I got my third DUI, I had no intention of stopping drinking. The judge told me I had two choices: 30 days in the workhouse or 90 days without alcohol and with 90 AA meetings. I'd done some time before, and didn't want to do any more—mostly because it interfered with my drinking. So I took option two, and started going to meetings. I had to get a meeting card filled out, so I could prove to the Probation Officer that I was going. I just sat and said nothing, fairly pissed off about having to be there. Nowhere on my radar was the goal of getting sober. I was only there for the judge.

But after a while, the things those AA people said starting sinking in. They told stories about themselves that made it damn near impossible to keep denying that I had a drinking problem. I still stayed dry because of the judge, but as the 90 days wore on, my girlfriend started saying how much more she loved me when I didn't drink. So after the 90 days was up, I kept going to meetings (and getting my card signed) for my girlfriend.

I went to meetings for about a year before I realized that I had started to be there—and be sober—for myself, not for the judge or my girl. It sounds weird to say, but that realization took me completely by surprise. Like I said, getting sober had never been my goal before—but suddenly it was now.

but instead to ask 'What now?'" There isn't much point in doing all this work to develop a positive attitude if we aren't going to build a better life with it. We now know how our past values, beliefs, and negative attitude have led us down a less-than-desirable life path. Look where we are now! The good news is that we can put positive beliefs, thoughts, and resulting actions to work today to plan a very desirable path for the rest of our lives.

If we're honest with ourselves, most of us have to admit that criminals are not the only people who fail because they don't take care of life's loose ends. At least some of the time, all of us struggle to follow through in relationships and at work. We have trouble attaining our goals because we drop the ball on important details.

The idea of setting future goals may seem to contradict our emphasis on living in the current seven seconds. In practice, these aren't mutually exclusive activities. When we acquire the habit of living in the now, we start to understand that life's challenges, life's opportunities—even life itself—becomes more interesting. The ideal life is not some immovable destination where we can arrive and say, "Ahhhhh."—but rather a journey where we often say, "Wow!"

It's more useful to think of a meaningful life as a journey that unfolds before us. It's smart to have a map to guide our trip, but it's also smart to be prepared for detours, surprises and beautiful vistas that don't appear on the map. Setting a goal is like creating our own personal map. This may seem more challenging than stopping by the highway rest area for one of those free state maps—but it's also a lot more fun!

We start our journey by imagining what goals we want to pursue. Imagining a goal starts with a dream: a desire for something we really want. Visualization of a goal (or anything else) is very powerful; it can direct our focus and channel our energies in ways we didn't think ourselves capable.

But a goal isn't really a goal until the dream has a date. How do we get this date? It requires a plan—our road map to our destination. Motivation is the fuel that takes us there. Setting goals allows us to set our priorities and determine a direction we want to go.

BrainGame: Examining Your Successes

Goal setting is more than just a practical way to aim for something like a better career. It's also a key to happiness because it puts us into action. Action can remove the blues in ways that logic or talking alone can't. Setting and pursuing a goal provides some other concrete benefits:

- Keeps us on track

- Forces us to establish a direction

- Improves our self-esteem as we achieve small accomplishments along the way

- Makes us aware of our weaknesses

- Makes us aware of our strengths

- Brings to mind past victories, which energizes our present state of mind

- Defines reality and separates it from wishful thinking

- Sets a standard for our decision-making process (e.g., we must say no to certain things and yes to others).

This is a self-reinforcing process that supports positive attitudes and builds positive habits. An established habit is tough and resilient. We all know an alcoholic or drug addict who can tell us (and show us!) how a habit can be much stronger than reason, love or other powerful forces.

That was more than 15 years ago, and I still go to meetings. Even though I have no legal obligation anymore, I still bring a PO attendance card and get it signed. Those little cards remind me of three things: 1) life is so much better than it was 15 years ago, 2) if I do something good for someone else's benefit (like a judge or a woman), I may end up doing something good for my own benefit and 3) my goals change as I go along—and my achievements often end up being much greater than anything I had imagined when I started.

—John H.

53

However, habit is not the same as rigidity. When mapping and traveling toward a goal, we need to remain willing to be flexible and resilient—qualities that Positive Attitude Development enhances!

BrainGame: Your Successes and Your Future

Meaningful living demands that we establish goals and set off in a good, orderly direction to achieve them.

You must decide what kind of person you want to BE before you know what to DO, which will determine what you will HAVE.

Summary

This lesson teaches how and why we should set goals to achieve meaningful living.

BrainGame

Examining Your Successes

Write down your thoughts about the questions below. Use another sheet of paper if you need it. After you've completed your answers, see page 76 to see some of our thoughts on the subject.

What is the difference between a goal and a wish?

_____

_____

Think of a time when you set a significant goal. Be specific and concrete in your answers. What was the goal?

_____

_____

What date did you set for attaining the goal?

_____

What obstacles did you have to overcome?

_____

What individuals, organizations and/or groups did you need to work with to accomplish the goal?

_____

What skills did you need?

_____

What was your plan?

_____

What was in it for you?

_____

_____

BrainGame

Your Successes and Your Future

Think of a significant goal you want to set for your future. Be specific and concrete in your answers. After you've completed your answers, see page 78 to see some of our thoughts on the subject.

What is the goal?

What date will you set for attaining the goal?

What obstacles will you have to overcome?

What individuals, organizations and/or groups will you need to work with to accomplish the goal?

What skills will you need?

What is your plan?

What's in it for you?

POSITIVE ATTITUDE DEVELOPMENT

DESTINY

Self-worth

We have what we seek. It is there all the time, and if we give it time, it will make itself known to us.

—Thomas Merton

I have value.

I deserve good friends.

I am not in this alone.

In this session:
· Who do I want to BE
· Will determine what I DO
· And what I will HAVE

How You Matter

SELF-WORTH IS NOT MANUFACTURED BY FACTS, situations or experience, but rather on how we evaluate those facts, situations and experiences. In part, self-worth is built on the feedback we get about our worth. We give ourselves some of that feedback. Other people give us feedback as well. We then interpret and evaluate what this feedback means about our concept of ourselves—our self-worth.

When we live out of a negative perspective, we give ourselves a poor sense of self worth. When we live with positive values, beliefs, attitude and thoughts, we give ourselves an enhanced sense of self worth.

When my prison sentence began, my self-worth was based on what I had and who I knew. Of course, upon entering prison, I lost nearly all of my physical possessions. Very soon, the people I knew began falling away from my life as well. Because my self-worth was so dependent on those external things and people, it deflated like a balloon and I didn't know how to refill it. Each time another

thing left my life, I descended deeper into a sense of worthlessness. As a result, I often struggled to get up in the morning and feel that I could accomplish anything that day.

After I went to prison, no one visited me—not even my brother or my fiancé. I kept hoping they would come and it hurt when they didn't. I joked that no one came because I had poor taste in friends. But deep inside, the empty visitors' room convinced me that I wasn't worth the trouble of visiting. It was nearly 12 years before I had another visitor.

But during those 12 years, I learned an important truth: Self-worth is not built on the quality of what I do or don't possess or what does or doesn't happen to me. Remember, self-worth is based on how I interpret those externals. The bottom line is that the quality of my personal possessions is beside the point. If I define myself by what I have or if I think the things I have are inferior, then I'll feel unworthy and be on my way to becoming an unlovable person.

Further reflection reveals that there are very few tangible things that can't be taken away from me. I can lose my car, my wife, my kids, my freedom—even an eye or kidney. But I will still be me. And I will still have potential to become more than I am right now (more useful to others, more compassionate, more positive), even if I lose my limbs or spend the rest of my days incarcerated. The potential I have is never inferior.

What about people who don't go to the extremes listed in The Self-worth Spiral? A great many people have what we might call a run-of-the-mill sense of self. Their self-worth is not too strong and not too weak, so they might seem to be in pretty good shape. But this is a case were the good is the enemy of the best. People like this are often like pinballs bouncing randomly around or sailboats without rudders. They fluctuate between feeling qualified and unqualified, appropriate and inappropriate. When presented with opportunity, they are uncertain and confused about their capability. While they may not feel that they deserve failure, they may also feel that they don't deserve to succeed, either.

It's a sad fact that many people go to their graves without ever making their unique contribution to the world. It's as if they misread the rhythms of their own possibilities and the measure of their own worth, so their music remains locked within, never added to the symphony of the universe.

After six months in prison, I started volunteering for the prison's positive attitude class just to kill time. I didn't pay that much attention to the class or my instructor role; I just went through the motions. One day, another inmate came up and told me, "Lyle, I'm trying to apply in my life some of the stuff you're teaching in that class. It really seems to be working!" I was shocked. I went back to my room and asked myself, "What does he mean? What did I do?"

...Whatsoever a man soweth, that shall he also reap.

—Galatians 6:7

I didn't find an answer, but I kept on helping to teach the class, working a little harder to present the things the guy said were working for him. A few weeks later, another inmate came up and thanked me for what I'd been teaching, saying it improved his life a lot.

I thought, "If it's working for these guys, maybe I should try it." So, it was really by accident that I started practicing these methods—even though (hypocritically) I was already preaching them.

I was happy with what I began to do, and even happier with the results I got. This was great, so I said, "I've got to do this again, to see if I'll feel the same way if I repeat the steps." I thought of it as a scientific experiment (after all, I was in prison after a career in underground chemistry!).

Repetition did work; the results were still wonderful. The experiments showed that I could trust this method and the universe. The pattern could be repeated with predictably reliable results. I could trust it because it worked—just like I can trust nature to freeze water at 0° C.

When I started having new awareness, trusting in the universe, thinking and living in the moment, having honesty, integrity, understanding, compassion, and love—then I started to enjoy what I put out into the world, and my self-worth started to build from within. My balloon started filling again.

But while our self-worth balloons may fill again, self-worth is not the same as self-inflation. Strong self-worth and meaningful living have their roots in humility. Humility requires understanding that we are one small part of the universe. In the big picture, one

human's individual part is not the most important force in the universe—even the president of the United States is less powerful than the forces that hold a tiny atom together.

While small, our place in the universe still has meaning. In other words, healthy self-worth requires the humility of balance—living without either grandiosity or self-abasement. Humility, awareness, integrity, compassion and all the rest give us greater understanding of the deep hurts in life—like the fact that no one came to visit me in prison.

I eventually realized the problem wasn't that I had poor taste in friends. The problem was that I had compartmentalized my friends and never fully committed to them. I had one group of friends to drink with, another to do drugs with, a third to go to the movies with, and so on. I was too busy being on the fly to do the steady, hard work of developing a deep bond with anyone.

My life was not integrated and my relationships with friends weren't deep and meaningful—to me or to them. My commitment was so weak that, if I'd been on the outside and one of them had been in prison, I probably wouldn't have visited him either. This was a sad reflection on how I led my life, but I could cope with that kind of new awareness because my sense of self was growing stronger and I was growing more resilient and compassionate. I loved that feeling because no one could take it away from me—except me.

Healthy self-worth allows us to live a life

> *Don't go around saying
> the world owes you a living.
> The world owes you nothing.
> It was here first.*
>
> **—Mark Twain**

that is not at war with ourselves or other people. The more secure our self-worth, the more inclined we are to treat others with respect, compassion and good will, because we don't perceive them as a threat to us. We don't feel like strangers, afraid in a world we never made. We begin to respect ourselves—and self-respect is the foundation of respect for others.

Self-worth grows through true, selfless service to people—including to ourselves. Such service is totally in our control, which means that our self-worth is also in our control. You can keep building it every day, making it more and more healthy and resilient. In fact, self-worth is like a muscle; if you don't exercise it every day, it atrophies.

If I continually reach out to others for love,

I am tipping forward, off center and unstable,

Leaning forward on whomever I contact,

And likely to fall flat and hard if the other
leaves.

If I continually withdraw in fear,

I am tipping backward, tense and rigid,

And the slightest surprise will push me over.

If I feel uncertain in myself

And unstable in my base,

Then all my contacts with others

Will be wobbly and lack conviction.

In contrast, if I can become centered and
balanced

In my own experience,

Then I can carry this moving center with me.

If I am balanced now,

Then I can move in any direction I wish

With no danger of falling,

And my contact with you is solid and real,

Coming to you from the root of my living.

—**Barry Stevens and John Stevens**
in *Embrace Tiger, Return to Mountain*
by Chunglaing Al Huang

Now this thought is going to come as a shocker!
The uncontrolled conscious mind of any individual
is little more than an open sewer which takes in all
manner of refuse and debris in the form of wrong
thoughts and feelings, along with the good

Unless you stand guard over what you take in, there
is no sifting, no filtering of the good from the bad.
It all goes into your inner consciousness. And what
goes in must eventually come out in the same form,
or remain within to attract more of the same....
because like always attracts like!

— Claude M. Bristol and Harold Sherman
TNT: The Power Within You

POSITIVE ATTITUDE DEVELOPMENT

Conclusion

WE'VE SPENT EIGHT SESSIONS TOGETHER in this PAD process, working on understanding the power of our Core Values, beliefs, attitude, thoughts, actions, habits, character, destiny, and the resulting quality of our lives. Here are two examples:

FIRST EXAMPLE: My life as an underground chemist:

My **Core Values** were:

> Instant gratification
>
> Power
>
> Greed

My **Beliefs** were:

> The one with the best drugs,
> most money
> and the most toys wins.

My **Attitude** was:

> I come first.
>
> I don't care about others.
>
> I don't trust anyone.

My **Thoughts** were:

> Get new clients
>
> Keep from getting busted
>
> Stop others stealing from me

My **Actions** were:

> Selling drugs
>
> Finding new clients
>
> Having more money

My **Habits** were:

> Distrusting
>
> Questioning everybody
>
> Watching for cops and detectives

My **Character** was:

> He's a user.
>
> He's a taker.
>
> He's a liar.

My **Destiny** was:

> Being arrested
>
> Loss of everything
>
> Incarceration

SUMMARY — My **Quality of Life** was:

> Hollow
>
> Helpless
>
> Hopeless

POSITIVE ATTITUDE DEVELOPMENT

SECOND EXAMPLE: My life as a Brain Coach:

My **Core Values** are:

> Transparency
>
> Wellness
>
> Compassion

My **Beliefs** are:

> Relationships are important.
>
> Relationships have quality.
>
> Lost relationships make me sad.

My **Attitude** is:

> Others are important.
>
> Others can be trusted.
>
> Others add quality to my life.

My **Thoughts** are:

> How can I be helpful?
>
> How can I be approachable?
>
> How can I live in the present?

My **Actions** are:

> Sharing my story
>
> Listening to other people's stories
>
> Being a constructive Brain Coach

My **Habits** are:

> Helping others feel valued
>
> Asking curious questions
>
> Trying to be non-judgmental

My **Character** is:

> He's a listener.
>
> He asks helpful questions.
>
> He cares about others.

My **Destiny** is:

> Trusted by others,
>
> A quality social network,
>
> And great memories.

SUMMARY — My **Quality of Life** is:

> Peaceful
>
> Meaningful
>
> Qualitative

My underground chemist Core Values will never produce the quality of life I now experience. More importantly, my Brain Coach Core Values will never cause me to become incarcerated again... ever.

BrainGame

Your Quality of Life

Reduce your final five Core Value cards to three. Now list your three Core Values and supporting beliefs, attitude, thoughts and actions... and your Quality of Life.

My **Core Values** are:

_____
_____
_____

My **Beliefs** are:

_____
_____
_____

My **Attitude** is:

_____
_____
_____

My **Thoughts** are:

_____
_____
_____

My **Actions** are:

_____
_____
_____

My **Habits** are:

_____
_____
_____

My **Character** is:

_____
_____
_____

My **Destiny** is:

_____
_____
_____

SUMMARY — My **Quality of Life** is:

_____
_____
_____

"I fully realize that no wealth or position can long endure,

unless built upon truth and justice; therefore,

I will engage in no transaction which does not benefit

all whom it affects. I will succeed by attracting to

myself the forces I wish to use, and the cooperation

of other people. I will induce others to serve me,

because of my willingness to serve others. I will

eliminate hatred, envy, jealousy, selfishness, and cynicism

by developing love for all humanity, because

I know that a negative attitude toward others

can never bring me success. I will sign my name

to this formula, commit it to memory and repeat

it once a day so that I can remain a self-reliant

and successful person."

— **Napoleon Hill**
Think and Grow Rich

Afterword

We hope that your life has been touched by our Positive Attitude Development process. We know PAD is not the only way to encounter the mystery of life, but it is one that has worked for thousands of prisoners—including lifers—many of them living in deep pain and despair.

It has transformed lives (including my own) and eliminated an emptiness that felt like it could never be filled. With this sense of fulfillment and the tools to recreate it daily, people like you and me have found bliss and beauty where we'd never seen it before—in the everydayness of life. May you enjoy this journey of discovery forever.

Thank you for participating in the PAD process.

—Lyle

Positive Attitude Development

Humor

Flexibility

Gratitude

Integrity

Patience

Understanding

Forgiveness

All rooted in Compassion

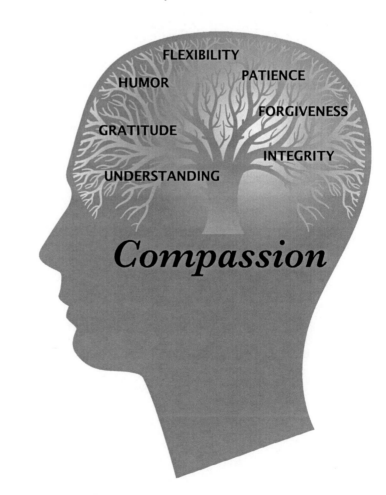

"What is an attachment? An emotional state of clinging caused by the belief that without some particular thing or some person you cannot be happy. This emotional state of clinging is composed of two elements, one positive and the other negative. The positive element is the flash of pleasure and excitement, the thrill that you experience when you get what you are attached to. The negative element is the sense of threat and tension that always accompanies the attachment."

— **Anthony de Mello**
The Way to Love

BrainGame Answers and Comments

Nine dot puzzle answer explanation

Most people find this puzzle impossible to solve. The reason is pretty simple—and illustrates how quickly and deeply a pattern of thinking gets lodged in our brains.

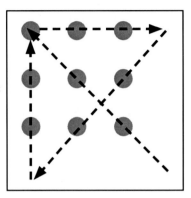

When we look at this puzzle, most of us (unconsciously) impose a square box on the picture—a box made from four invisible lines along the "edge" of the puzzle. Thinking this way about the situation, we develop the belief that we can't draw any lines outside of that invisible square. But as you can see the solution requires that we extend some of the lines beyond the invisible box we imposed. To quote the old cliché, we have to "think outside the box."

We can work on the puzzle for hours, demonstrating tons of good will, determination and persistence. Those qualities are positive and admirable, but, on their own, they are inadequate to the situation. That's because our "we have to stay inside the (invisible) box" thinking and beliefs make it impossible to connect all nine dots with only four straight lines. We can't solve the puzzle using our existing pattern of thinking.

This puzzle is a simple illustration of why it's so important for us to develop new beliefs, attitudes, and thoughts—so we have more capacity to successfully deal with the new and surprising situations life has in store for us.

p. 24

BrainExercise: What Are *You* Thinking?

What's the first thought that comes to mind when you see each of these words?
Here are some common examples I heard from other PAD participants.

Anger: Someone's always pushing my buttons. People make me mad. It's someone else's fault.

Betrayal: Unfair. The story of my life. Abandonment. Why I'm in this mess in the first place.

Joy: It's not really possible. Joy is fake and never real. Getting high.

Compassion: To walk a mile in another person's shoes.

Forgiveness: I deserve it but others don't. You can't forgive and forget. Some things you just can't ever forgive.

Here are some alternative ways to think about these words:

Anger: The cork that keeps every other emotion stuffed inside. Anger is my choice—no one can make me mad. Anger is an understandable first response—but dangerously corrosive to hang onto over time.

Betrayal: Violation of trust. Betrayal will happen to me (since people are imperfect) but that doesn't mean I'm abandoned by everyone. What looks and feels like betrayal may be something less serious (like simple thoughtlessness). Betrayal can be information to help me know who I can really trust.

Joy: I can feel joy here and now. It does exist. I can be happy and have good times, no matter what the circumstances.

Compassion: Other people have value. Compassion is always nonviolent.

Forgiveness: A process, not an event. Forgiving is difficult (but not impossible) and, ultimately, always necessary to achieve freedom and happiness.

What do you think it means to begin a new life?

PAD demonstrates that we can re-create our lives and change our destiny if and when we begin to adjust our beliefs, attitudes, thoughts and actions.

How can you begin a new life in prison?

By choosing to develop new habits and arrest any negative thinking. The decision to do this is NOT dependent on my surroundings or circumstances.

Do you need to forget the past to begin a new life?

No. But we do need to discard the belief that our past completely determines our present and future. The past can inform our present and provide clues for what to do—and not do—in order to improve our present and future.

How important is forgiveness in beginning a new life?

Forgiveness is essential for creating a new life. Without it, we remain stuck in the past and its old thinking patterns. But forgiving usually requires changing our values, beliefs, attitude and thoughts. In fact, applying PAD methods to our memories of past events can actually change how we interpret their meaning today.

Are there any actions that you just can't forgive? If so, what are they?

We believe it is possible to forgive anything—and that the act of forgiving past violations is in our hands, not anyone else's. To forgive requires only one person. Forgiving doesn't mean we condone someone else's wrong actions—but it does mean we stop choosing to have those actions control any part of our lives today. True forgiveness brings liberation because, as a sage once said, "Resentment is the sword with which we pierce our own souls." However, it is very difficult to forgive past actions if we maintain the same old Core Values and beliefs. On the other hand, forgiveness of someone else is ultimately a gift we give to ourselves.

What purpose does it serve to bury the hatchet if you're going to mark the spot?

None (I bet that answer didn't surprise you!). If you keep returning to a past violation in your mind or conversations, that's evidence that you haven't finished the forgiveness process—and you haven't freed yourself from your pattern of resenting and feeling "controlled" by past events. Marking the spot where you buried the hatchet is the first step on a path to going back and repeating old behaviors. If nothing changes, nothing changes.

If we don't learn from the past are we condemned to repeat it?

Yes. If we don't learn from our mistakes we will keep repeating them and keep getting the same old outcomes. Just remember that popular definition of insanity: doing the same thing over and over, yet expecting different results.

p. 29
BrainExercise

Write out the words associated with the letters below.

S.	Susceptible	S.	Susceptible
N.	Negative	P.	Positive
I.	Influences	I.	Influences
O.	Other	O.	Other
P.	People	P.	People

How did Morris Goodman repel SNIOP in his recovery?

He didn't let his beliefs, thoughts and actions be determined by what the professionals around him thought, believed or did. He chose not to accept or internalize a paradigm that said he couldn't recover.

Morris put himself on a strict mental diet—but it wasn't a diet of deprivation. What kind of nourishment did Morris feed his brain while on his mental diet?

He feed his brain positive, hopeful, expectant, and constructive thoughts. He also reached out to bring positive, hopeful, expectant, and constructive people (like his sister) close by to support him.

Give some examples of negative influence you have to overcome in prison.

Here are some common examples from other PAD participants.

> People saying I'd be back.
> People saying that I would never amount to anything.
> People saying I couldn't be successful with my past.
> The negative influences of prison.
> The belief I would never find a good job or relationship.

What negative influences if any, will you experience after your release?

Here are some common answers I heard while teaching PAD.

> People expecting me to fail.
> People who complain but never change.
> People not willing to give an ex-con a chance.
> People who give up to stay where they are, instead of giving up to move on.
> My own thinking patterns when I'm not vigilant about keeping my beliefs, attitude and thoughts positive.

p. 30

BrainExercise: Beliefs, Thoughts and Actions

What do you think would have happened to you if you had been in an accident like Morris Goodman had?

Here's the most common answer I heard while teaching. "I would have given up and died." But I'm not convinced that's what most of us would actually do. For example, I was in a serious auto accident several years before I went to prison. I was pronounced dead shortly after arrival. Even without fully understanding what I was doing, I believed in the power of my thinking. I knew there was a way out of that mess and that I wouldn't give up. I didn't give up and eventually I recovered. On the down side, the surgery and recovery exposed me for the first time to life altering chemicals (triggering an unhealthy fascination with them)—but the point is that we often have more capacity for survival and recovery than we realize.

What would your beliefs, attitudes and thoughts have been in that situation?

Here is an answer I heard while teaching PAD.

The odds are too great and the doctors are right. I would give up and die.

What is the difference between those beliefs, attitudes and thoughts and the ones that Morris seems to have in his recovery?

Instead of giving up or giving in to negative beliefs, attitudes and thoughts, Morris chose another path. He believed in the power of his thoughts. He believed that he could overcome situations like a serious illness and that circumstance alone would not dictate his future.

p. 33
BrainExercise: Zeroing in on Now

Here's one example of the thoughts a PAD participant had during a 10-second period:

This is silly.

I'm hungry.

Where is my girlfriend?

My foot itches.

Will I get a letter today?

Is time up yet?

I want coffee.

p. 34
BrainExercise: Fear Factors

How do you define fear?

F. alse	F. antasized
E. vidence	E. xperiences
A. ppearing	A. ppearing
R. eal	R. eal

Describe a time when false or fantasized experiences appeared real in your life.

Here are some examples from past PAD participants:

When I thought someone's facial expression or tone of voice meant they were mad at me.

When I was convinced that my wife was cheating on me, even though she really wasn't.

When I thought a guard was coming after me, when it turned out that he was just walking by.

If you knew you were going to die tonight what would you do with the rest of today?

Some examples from past PAD participants:

I'd get as high as I could or have as much sex as I could.

I would keep living my normal life because I believe it contains the quality of life I enjoy and want.

How would your loved ones describe you at your funeral?

Some examples from past PAD participants:

My dad was never home.

My dad spent a lot of time in prison.

My dad was mean to mom and all of us.

p. 38

BrainExercise

How are you tested or challenged every day?

All of us are challenged by changes that happen to one degree or another every day. We can be challenged by another person's behavior, like believing that a friend has betrayed us or that our business partner wants to cut us loose. We are tested every day in our journey to reshape our beliefs, attitude, thinking and behaviors.

Certain words or phrases promote failure. What words or phrases have you heard other people use that you think have promoted failure in their lives?

Some examples from past PAD participants:

I can't, I quit, yes, but…, no use trying, unable, cannot, impossible, out of the question, failure, hopeless situation, improbable, not me, not my problem, never been done before.

What words or phrases have you used that may promoted failure in your life?

Some examples from past PAD participants:

(See the answers to the last question!)

What things do you tell yourself that erode your motivation?

I don't know how to do this. It's never been done before. I'm too old. People don't care anyway. It's a waste of time. If it was possible, someone else would have done it already.

What words or phrases do you need to remove from your vocabulary to help you reach your goals?

The best place to start is by removing the phrases you listed in the last three questions. Use those lists to help police your thinking.

Which of these statements do you believe?
The correct answer is B. Failure is not genetic. It is a learned behavior—which means we can change it by shifting to positive beliefs, attitudes, and thoughts.

p. 39

BrainExercise: Determining Your Success

What have you given up on in the past that, upon reflection, you could have accomplished if you'd persisted?
Some common answers include:

> A relationship
>
> Reading a book
>
> Winning a competition
>
> Finishing high school
>
> Finishing college

What are some small steps you've taken to reach a goal?
This list might include things like:

> Set a date to accomplish my goal
>
> Listed the obstacles I have to overcome
>
> Listed the groups, organizations, and individuals I can (or have to) work with
>
> Listed the skills necessary
>
> Made a daily, weekly, and monthly plan
>
> Listed why I want this goal

What's a positive way to perceive obstacles and adversity?
Obstacles and adversity are inevitable, no matter what our situation. Rather than resenting them, it helps to see them as opportunities and challenges which can help motivate taking steps toward success.

Is life like the Super Bowl—does your winning depend on someone else losing?
No. Think about it like a parent. Making one of your kids fail is not the way to help another of your kids to succeed. The more people I help become successful the more successful I will become.

What other ways might there be to perceive success?

>   The feeling you have accomplished something worth while

>   Identifying success before you start your journey

>   A happy relationship with your partner and a well integrated family

>   Being of service to others, without expecting any reward

>   Doing the right thing when no one is watching

p. 41

BrainExercise: Tracking Your Personal Development

What are examples of what you've learned in some of the peaks and valleys of your life?

Peaks: Just as in hard times, when it comes to good times, this too shall pass. That means enjoy and appreciate the peaks as they happen. The memory and inspiration of life's peaks can sustain me in the valleys. There is always something for which to be grateful in life—including life itself.

Valleys: This too shall pass. Important life lessons for personal growth happen in the valleys. In the valleys, I have learned that persistence is important. Trust is the key for creativity and resilience. Life has never given me more that I can handle, but sometimes it has taken all I have. And that's OK.

p. 55

BrainExercise: Examining Your Successes

What is the difference between a goal and a wish?

A goal has a date for it to be accomplished. A wish is just a statement.

Think of a time when you set a significant goal. Be specific and concrete in your answers. What was the goal?

Some goals that past PAD participants listed include:

>   To read 50 pages of nonfiction everyday

>   To complete (and do well in) a course

>   To develop a relationship with a life partner who has similar Core Values

>   To write a book

>   To learn carpentry

What date did you set for attaining the goal?
The choices can run any realistic length of time:

> By the end of each day

> By the end of the year

> In five years' time

What obstacles did you have to overcome?

> My laziness and finding the books

> Family objections or apathy

> The urge to get into a relationship with the first person I met

> Uncooperative guards, staff

What individuals, organizations and/or groups did you need to work with to accomplish the goal?

> Friends who could share their books with me

> The library staff

> Chaplains, AA/NA group leaders and other volunteers

> People who can supplement my skills or teach me the skills I need

> Educators

What skills did you need?
Past PAD participants listed things like:

> I had to learn to read and concentrate in spite of noises

> Learned how to improve the curriculum of my class

> I had to learn to directly ask for—and accept—help from others

What was your plan?
Past PAD participants listed things like:

> I determined to read three times during every day

> Practice, practice, practice

> Become friends with someone before thinking about getting romantically involved with them

What was in it for you?
Past PAD participants listed things like:

Peace of mind and knowledge that no one could take it from me

A way to expand my horizons

Enjoy a wonderful relationship

p. 56

BrainExercise: Your Successes and Your Future

Think of a significant goal you want to accomplish. Be specific and concrete in your answers.

Below is my own example of how I set and managed the goal of developing the PAD course in prison—and for after my release.

What is the goal?

I want to help others challenge their belief systems and thus change the way they see the world.

What date will you set for attaining the goal.

I have set a series of short term goals. I will have my book published before the end of 2008.

I will have a web site developed by Nov. 2008.

I will have an e-learning video completed by Jan. 2009.

What obstacles will you have to overcome?

I will have to generate enough funding to complete this task.

I will have to find the right people to help me.

I will have to practice so I am the best at what I do.

What individuals, organizations and/or groups will you need to work with to accomplish the goal?

A web-based learning service

Men as Peacemakers

A professional writer

Positive Attitude Development Group

Corporations and NGOs

Local leaders

What skills will you need?

Public speaking skills

Speech writing skills

Communication skills

What is your plan?

To follow all of the steps laid out above

What's in it for you?

I will feel that my life is more meaningful because I will have changed the world for the better. I will continue to grow along my own journey of Positive Attitude Development by practicing and working on it every day. I will be of service to others.

Acknowledgments

The author is deeply grateful to the following people, and many others unnamed, for their help in bringing to reality this book and the Positive Attitude Development process.

John and Lyn Clark Pegg	Joe Kelly	Leo and Cathy Piatz
Tom Halloran	Paul LeRose	Ruth Stricker
Jeff Jurkens	Christopher Motter	Whole Person Associates

For more information, visit
www.wildesbraincoach.com

or email

Lyle@wildesbraincoach.com